My Journey of Molestation and Rape and How I Overcame

I've overcome darkness, and now
I'm walking in His Light!

Renee C Thomas

My Journey of Molestation and Rape and How I Overcame

Copyright © 2025 by Renee C Thomas

All rights reserved. No part of this book may be reproduced or transmitted in any form or by any means, electronic or mechanical, including photocopying, recording, or by any information storage and retrieval system, without permission in writing from the author.

Scripture quotations are taken from the Holy Bible, the New Living Translation, and the New International Version, used by permission.

For information, contact Renee Thomas, mrsthomas07@gmail.com

Cover Designed by ChatGPT

ISBN: 9798993223964 (Paperback)

Made in the USA

First Edition: October 2025

Contents

Preface	
Introduction	1
Molestation	3
Grey Rape	7
How I Overcame	10
My Life Now	12
Trauma	14
Take a Moment to think about your own Journey	16
Scriptures to Speak over Yourself	18
Prayer	19
From my Healing to Helping Others	20
Acknowledgement	21

Preface

It's Time to Release

This book was written because I said **yes** to God. For years, I carried the weight of silence, shame, and embarrassment, but God told me it's time for me to release it all. Writing this is the final step of my healing journey, but it's also a calling to help others who are still holding their pain in secret.

It's time for me to push past fear and allow my story to speak life into someone else's. My journey hasn't been easy, but it's proof that healing is possible. What happened to me shaped me, but it didn't define me; God does. I pray that others find the courage to face their truth, release their pain, and begin their own journey toward freedom and peace.

Introduction

My name is Renee Thomas, I'm sharing my story because there are so many people that's been molested or grey raped who are silently hurting and battling the trauma that comes with it, and don't know it, and they feel like they're fine, but they're not. I was 33 years old when I had an emotional breakdown because of the molestation, and I had to seek counseling, which was Hypnotherapy.

Starting at the age of 6 or 7, I was molested by my grandpa. At the age of 29, I was grey raped by a guy I was getting to know. Because of the traumatic experiences that I never shared with anyone and kept my emotions and feelings internal, my brain pushed the molestation to the side so it wouldn't haunt me, and block the rape. My brain was trying to protect me, but it's causing me to have memory loss, and I don't know if I'll ever receive my memories back.

I started having daytime blackouts or short-term memory loss, where I would forget what I did seconds or a minute ago. I went back to my Hypnotherapist, and he unblocked a memory of me being grey raped.

Because of these traumatic experiences, I was ashamed, embarrassed, I felt guilty, I was fearful of anyone knowing, I isolated myself from family and friends, I had low self-esteem, I didn't feel like anyone loved me, and I had an unforgiving heart towards myself, family members, other people, and the men who molested and raped me.

It's time for women and men to find their voice and speak their truth. Molestation is a generational curse, and it's time to break it. It's time for families to stop sweeping molestation under the rug and start believing their loved ones who are trying to let them know someone is touching them. My experience was different; I didn't say a word because it was our little secret.

This book is my truth and tells my story of how I remember the events, and it has explicit details.

Molestation

My grandpa woke me up in the middle of the night to follow him upstairs to his bedroom. I had to take my clothes off and lie on the floor. He would use his hands and tongue to fondle my vagina until I had a sensation, an orgasm, but he didn't stop; he kept going until he was finished. Once he was finished, I put my clothes on, and before I went back to bed, he would say, 'This is our little secret.' The next day, I would sit on the toilet longer than normal because it hurt and stung my vagina when I peed. At the time, my family and I lived in Chicago, so this happened every weekend I would visit my grandparents, and during the summer months after we moved back to Mississippi.

When my grandmother died and my grandpa remarried, he stopped molesting me, but he would ask me if I remembered our little secret, and I would say no, hoping he wouldn't start back. The last summer, I visited my grandpa, he stuck his hands down my pants, and I was of age to tell the secret, but I chose not to. I knew right from wrong, but I also knew that if I shared, it was going to damage the relationship between a dad and his daughter, and our family. I don't know if it had anything to do with the fact that I didn't have a relationship with my dad, and I wanted that relationship, so I didn't want to ruin their relationship.

I was 15 or 16 when my mom found out that I had been molested. My grandpa molested another family member, which led to her asking me, and I told her yes.

I never blame my mom for what happened to me; I kept that secret. She gave me the option to go to counseling, but I refused because I felt like I was fine. After all, my brain pushed the memories to the side so they wouldn't haunt me.

The Effects of Being Molested

Molestation experiences deep emotional effects that aren't always obvious.

Physical Effect

As I got older, I started having a desire for the sensation, an orgasm, which caused me to do things that I was ashamed of and felt guilty about.
- I fondle myself.
- I let cousins fondle me.
- Other people and I would hunch with our clothes on, boys and girls.
- I let a teenage boy I had just met play inside of me.
- In high school, I chose to hang out with my boyfriend instead of my friends. It wasn't him that I chose, it was the sensation that he was giving me.

My body wasn't betraying me; it was reacting to something it didn't understand. The body can respond to touch even when the heart and mind don't want it; it was confused due to the trauma of molestation.

Emotional Effect

As a child, I didn't know how to feel, as a teenager, I didn't know how to feel, and as an adult, I didn't know how to feel. I was emotionally numb, but I had
- Trust issues

- Low self-esteem
- I would binge eat, not really knowing why.
- I isolated myself from family and friends.
- I felt like I wasn't good enough or worthy of love.
- I had affection for men who gave me attention.
- I was ashamed and embarrassed by the things I did.

For a long time, I didn't realize how much being molested changed me on the inside. I thought the pain was only about what happened to my body, but it was deeper. I carried feelings I didn't have words for. I smiled when I was hurting, I said, "I'm fine", when I wasn't. I didn't know what I was feeling was connected to my trauma of molestation.

Mental Effect
I remembered what happened to me, but it never bothered me, so I thought. My brain pushed the memory of the molestation to the side because it thought it was protecting me, but at the same time, it started blocking other memories. But even though I didn't think anything was wrong with me, molestation was affecting my body, emotions, and life in different ways.
- I wanted the sexual sensation, an orgasm, but I couldn't understand why.
- Without some of my memories, I felt like I didn't know who I was; a part of me was missing.
- Self-doubt, feeling like I was crazy because I couldn't remember certain things or a lot of my childhood.
- I had a strong, strange reaction to smoke because my grandpa smoked.

My brain pushed my memory to the side for survival; my mind did what it had to do to let me live, but the mental effects were still there.

Grey Rape

Anonymous and I just went on our first day date. Later that night, I didn't have anything going on, so I went to his house to chill and watch a movie. I just wanted to get to know him more. We made margaritas and watched a movie. I know how much liquor I can take, but he kept insisting I add more liquor to my margarita and share some of his with me because he had three times as much liquor in his margarita. He made my last margarita for the night.

When I was ready to leave, I was so dizzy and drunk I couldn't leave. This was the first time in my life I felt this way. He only had one room with one bed, so I lay down in the bed with my clothes on. He stood over me and said, "I know you didn't come all this way to just chill and watch a movie". He took my pants off, and I couldn't do anything but lie there and let him have sex with me. Sex was not on my mind when I went to his house. I woke up in the middle of the night and left.

On my way home, I was confused about the situation and didn't know what to do. I didn't want to talk to anyone because I was embarrassed and felt guilty, as a grown woman, for putting myself in this type of situation. Of all people, I should know better.

Why Grey Rape?
First, I want to say rape is rape. I call it Grey Rape because it was not consensual, but I didn't fight back or say no.

The Effects of Being Raped

Pain shows up in behaviors, thoughts, or relationships, not realizing they come from being raped.

Mental Effect

I was so emotional and kept what happened to me internal, and eventually, my brain blocked the rape.

I started having daytime blackouts.
- I could be doing something simple like exercising, cooking, or cleaning, and suddenly realized I had no memory of what I'd just done.
- I could remember what I was doing before and after, but that one small moment disappeared, like it never happened.

I thought I was losing my mind. Hypnotherapy helped me figure out what was going on and made me realize that I was still carrying pain that I never processed.

Emotional Effect

Before my mind blocked this trauma, I was an emotional wreck, but I kept it to myself. I felt
- Confused
- Guilty
- Self-Doubt
- Shame
- Embarrassed
- Fear
- I started binge eating

Even though I was emotionally confused about the situation, I stayed in a relationship with Anonymus. I feel like it goes back to being molested

He gave me that sensation, an organism that my body yearned for.

Physical Effect
There were no visible marks, but I had pain in my pelvic area.

How I Overcame

God
I never blamed God for what people did to me or the choices I made.
- I prayed for change, and he placed hypnotherapy in my spirit years before I finally decided to go.
- I read scripture and spoke them over myself.

Luke 17:14 (NIV) When he saw them, he said, "Go, show yourselves to the priests." And as they went, they were cleansed.

They weren't healed immediately; it came as they walked.

In the same way, as I walked with the Lord, I had to face and endure the suffering of my past. My healing didn't happen all at once; it came in steps. Each step led to a breakthrough, and every step brought me closer to healing.

Therapy
A friend asked me, "How would I know if my daughter has been touched/molested?" I broke down, I had an emotional breakdown, so I didn't have any option but to seek help. I chose Hypnotherapy because I wasn't ready to talk about what happened or relive the details out loud, but I needed help.

Hypnotherapy helped me
- Unblocked memories that my brain blocked.
- Release shame, embarrassment, guilt, fear, and self-doubt.
- Release emotions that I didn't know I had.
- Realize I was isolating myself from people.
- Realize I had unforgiving emotions from family and friends who wronged me growing up.
- Stop binge eating
- Realize I needed to love myself.
- I was carrying pain I didn't cause

Healing didn't happen at once; I had to peel back layers of pain every time I chose to face what once had me broken, chained, and bound.

Forgiveness

Forgiveness was not easy. I needed to forgive myself for staying silent, for doing all the sexual activities I did to myself, for allowing other people to touch me, my grandpa for molesting me, and the guy who raped me.

Forgiveness didn't excuse what happened to me or make me forget. I released the weight of my brokenness and trauma and gave it to God. He restored my soul, and now I'm free.

My Life Now

I have never been happier. I'm doing things I never thought I would. It feels amazing to notice the change happening within me. About a year before I wrote this book, I had a dream. In the dream, I was standing in a gas station, nobody was there but me and a cashier; it was empty, gray, and lifeless. That gas station represented my old life: empty, lonely, and drained. Then I opened a door and stepped into another space, which was full of people, colorful, and lively. That's my life now: full of abundance, joy, and purpose.

Today, I have a personal relationship with God. I knew Him before, but now I know Him deeply. My heart has truly opened to Him, and because of that, I'm able to open it to others.

I no longer isolate myself from people. When I'm invited to a family event, I make sure I go and participate. Because of isolation, I isolated myself from my sister, which wasn't my intention because I wanted a relationship with her, but I was never there for her. After therapy, I reached out and apologized for not being there, and now I must wait until she forgives me and is ready to have a relationship with me.

For a long time, I wanted friends, but I wasn't showing myself to be friendly. Then, right after I forgave my grandfather, God sent a new friend into my life.

Our connection was immediate and genuine, and I know it wasn't anybody but God. I also joined a Bible study group with an amazing group of women. At first, I was hesitant and full of self-doubt, but once again, God pushed me beyond my comfort zone and placed me exactly where I needed to be.

What once felt like an ending was really the beginning of the life God had planned for me all along.

Trauma

Trauma is more than just a painful event; it's the deep emotional, mental, and sometimes physical wound left behind after something overwhelms a person's ability to cope. It can come from abuse, neglect, violence, or any experience that leaves someone feeling powerless, unsafe, or unloved.

When trauma happens, especially in childhood, it doesn't just fade away with time. It becomes stored in the mind, body, and heart, shaping how a person sees themselves and the world around them.

As a **child**, trauma can steal innocence and safety. A child may grow up feeling afraid, confused, or ashamed, even when they can't explain why. They might learn to hide their emotions, distrust adults, or believe the lie that what happened was their fault.

When that wounded child becomes a **teenager**, the pain often shows up in different ways: anger, rebellion, isolation, or searching for love in unsafe places. Many teens silently battle depression, anxiety, or low self-worth without realizing it's connected to what happened years before.

By the time that child grows into an **adult**, the trauma may still influence their choices, relationships, and self-image.

It can lead to cycles of brokenness; difficulty trusting others, fear of intimacy, or constant emotional exhaustion.

With awareness, therapy, healing, and faith, trauma can be faced and transformed.

Take a moment to think about your own journey

Sometimes what we call "attitude," "fear," or "overthinking" is really an old wound still asking to be healed. Healing begins when you stop running from the pain and start listening to what it's been trying to tell you.

- What moments from your childhood or past still make you feel uneasy or emotional when you think about them?

- Have you ever minimized your pain or told yourself to "just get over it"?

- Do you allow yourself to feel, or do you shut down when emotions rise?

- How have your past experiences shaped the way you see yourself and trust others?

- Are there people, places, or memories you avoid because they bring up feelings you don't want to face?

- In what ways do you see your past pain showing up in your relationships, choices, or self-talk today?

- What does healing look like for you, and what's one small step you can take toward it right now?

- What's stopping you from sharing your story?

Your voice carries healing, and God is with you wherever you go.

Joshua 1:9 (NIV) Be strong and courageous. Do not be afraid; do not be discouraged, for the Lord your God will be with you wherever you go.

Healing starts when you decide to no longer let the pain control your present. Releasing what happened doesn't mean forgetting or saying it was okay; it means choosing freedom over bondage. Take one step at a time; you don't start with having all the answers. It starts with having the courage to take the first step.

Start journaling your feelings, pray honestly to God, talk with someone you trust, and seek therapy. Remember, release is a process, not a moment. Each time you let go of a piece of the pain, you make more room for peace, joy, and purpose. You survived what tried to destroy you; now it's time to walk in the freedom and purpose God created for you.

Trauma may have shaped who you are, but it will not define who you become.

Scriptures to Speak over Yourself

Psalm 147:3 (NIV) He heals the brokenhearted and binds up their wounds.
- God is healing every broken place in me that still hurts.

Jeremiah 30:17 (NIV) But I will restore you to health and heal your wounds, declares the Lord,
- The Lord is restoring me and healing my brokenness.

1 Peter 5:7 (NIV) Cast all your anxiety on him because he cares for you.
- I give God my shame, guilt, embarrassment, fears, and anxiety because He cares for me.

Psalm 55:22 (NIV) Cast your cares on the Lord and he will sustain you; He will never let the righteous be shaken.
- God is sustaining me as I release my trauma to Him.

John 1:5 (NIV) The light shines in the darkness, and the darkness has not overcome it.
- God's light is shining in every dark place in my life, and the darkness cannot stop my healing.

Prayer

Heavenly Father, I lift up the person reading these words right now. You know their heart, their story, and the weight they've been carrying. You see the silent tears, the hidden pain, and the desire for something new. Lord, meet them right where they are.

Give them the encouragement to release what's been holding them back: fear, shame, guilt, embarrassment, and doubt. Remind them that change doesn't start with perfection; it starts with surrender. Wrap them in Your love so tightly that they no longer seek comfort in what once hurt them.

Father, open their eyes to see that they are worthy of peace, healing, and joy. Let them know that this moment is not the end; it's the beginning of a new chapter You've written for them.

Restore their hope, renew their strength, and transform their heart to reflect Your grace.

May they walk boldly into the light of freedom, knowing that You are with them every step of the way. In Jesus name, Amen.

From my Healing to Helping Others

Renee's Ministry

Renee's Ministry exists to help anyone who is battling the pain of molestation or rape. If you need someone to talk to, pray with, or simply listen without judgment, I want you to know that I am here for you.

I am not a licensed counselor, but I can share guidance from my own healing journey and, when the Lord leads, offer encouragement and wisdom inspired by Him. If you need, I can also help you find professional counseling or local resources.

You can contact me anytime via Messenger on Renee's Ministry Facebook page or by email at mrsthomas07@gmail.com. When you write, please include your name, a little about yourself, what you're currently facing, and the best way to contact you.

I understand the importance of privacy and trust. Everything that's shared will remain confidential.

Remember, you are not alone. God sees you, loves you, and cares deeply for your healing. Sometimes, He places people in our lives to walk beside us on the journey.

Acknowledgement

I want to thank my husband and mom for their love and support. Sharing my story was not easy, but it was necessary for my healing and growth. Your encouragement gave me the strength to keep going when it was hard to face my past. Thank you for believing in me, standing beside me, and reminding me that my voice matters. I love y'all with all my heart.

om/pod-product-compliance